LIONEL MESSI

TO THE TOP!

2012 Sets a record for most goals scored in a La Liga season, with 50.

2011 Returns to win Spain's Super Cup in the 2010-2011 season.

2010 Wins Spain's Super Cup in the 2009-2010 season.

2009 Wins the King's Cup in 2008-2009 season.

2008 Is named captain of FC Barcelona, and wears the number 10 jersey for the first time.

2007 Plays on the senior team in the American Cup Venezuela 2007.

2006 Plays on Argentina's senior team play in the 2006 World Cup Germany.

2005 Obtains citizenship from Spain on September 25, which allows him to register as a soccer player in the European community.
Wins the World Cup Under 20 joining the Argentinean National Team on July 2. Is recognized as the best goalie and player of the tournament.
Scores his first professional goal and at the age of 17, becomes the youngest player to score for FC Barcelona in the Spanish League.

2004 Plays his first official match with FC Barcelona jersey on October 16.

2003 Plays his first friendly match joining FC Barcelona official team on November 16.

2000 Arrives to Spain on September 17. On the following day he begins his tryouts at FC Barcelona.

1995 Is diagnosed with growth hormone problems.

1994 Is officially registered at the club Newell's Old Boys on March 21.

1987 Lionel Andrés Messi is born on June 24.

ISBN-13: 978-1-4222-2659-9 (hc) — 978-1-4222-9200-6 (ebook)

Printing (last digit) 9 8 7 6 5 4 3 2 1
Printed and bound in the United States of America.
CPSIA Compliance Information: Batch #S2013. For further
information, contact Mason Crest at 1-866-MCP-Book.

About the Author: Carlos Sosa was born in Buenos Aires on March 3, 1972. He is an Argentinean sports journalist with a long history covering events for various national and international publications. Although he has covered many different sports, he specializes in soccer and hockey.

Photo credits: EFE / Ed Oudenaarden: 13; Shutterstock.com: 1, 2, 4, 7, 8, 10, 11, 14, 16, 17, 19, 20, 22, 23, 24, 25, 26, 29, 30; UNICEF: 28.

TABLE OF CONTENTS

Lionel Messi is one of only three players who have won the FIFA Golden Ball three times during his career.

CHAPTER 1

A Star Is Born in Rosario

WHEN Lionel "Leo" Messi first appeared on the field, it seemed as though he could perform magic with the ball. He often leaves fans speechless. Messi has won many titles and awards. Although he has not been playing for long, today his name is synonymous with soccer around the world.

Lionel Messi was born in Rosario, Argentina, on June 24, 1987. The Messi family does not have a notable sporting history or a past related to the high-level sport. Celia Cuccitini, his mother, was a working woman and housewife, and his father, Jorge Messi, was an employee of a factory in the city.

Lionel Messi was born to a family in which his two older brothers, Rodrigo and Matias, were already accustomed to playing soccer. Some years after the birth of Leo, Maria Sol, the youngest sister, would complete the family of six and become a central part of his life.

His uncles, cousins and grandparents have also been very involved in his life. The Cuccitini-Messi family is one of those families that share a big dinner on Sundays, where they communicate the latest news of their respective lives with each other. From his family Leo found the self-control, support, and calm needed in order for him to do his best daily.

Play by Play

Leo has enjoyed playing soccer since he could remember. As for many thousands of children in Argentina, soccer is

They say that Celia, Lionel Messi's maternal grandmother, was the first one to discover his talent with the ball. She was the one who brought him for the very first time to Grandoli to play with his brothers. One day one of the players on his older brothers' team was missing and Leo's grandmother told the coach to put Leo in. Reluctantly, the coach obeyed. He could not believe his eyes—Leo had magic, and nobody could stop him with the ball. Celia was not fortunate enough to see Leo succeed as a professional, but she is always present in his memories. He has said that she is a kind of guardian angel, who helps him in difficult times.

forever a part of one's daily routine. Soccer is the most popular Argentinean sport. In order to learn how to play, one only needs to go out on the sidewalks and the opportunity will certainly present itself.

In Argentina one lives and breathes soccer in the town squares, in the schoolyards and on the street. It is common when a child learns to walk, he is given a ball and his parents help him to kick with his little feet, while shouting "goal!"

But Argentinean children do not need a football to enjoy this game. A can, a roll of toilet paper, or an orange are sufficient for the little game to appear. The afternoon sun and time in the open fields have been the breeding ground to form the greatest Argentinean soccer players.

Neighborhood Soccer

The Messi family was part of Grandoli, a neighborhood private team created by its residents. The idea that mobilized the team was simple: give children the opportunity to play sports with friends after school.

And it was there, where Leo began playing soccer. His skill and speed with the ball remainins in the memory of those who had the chance to see him in those earlier days.

Soccer Club

Before reaching the age of six, Leo was already the star of Grandoli. His skills with ball made one believe he was born to succeed. Back in those days he was affectionately called "Pulga" (flea) or "Pulguita" (little flea), because he was one of the smallest players on the team but was unparalleled in his agility and speed.

In those days, his older brothers played for a famous team in the city of Rosario called "Newell's Old Boys." One day Leo substituted for one of the missing players. The coaches immediately made him a member of the squad. It was 1994 and Leo was playing on one of the best teams in the city. He was not yet 7 years old.

Leo's parents say he was a mischievous child who always wanted to win at whatever he did. He did not like school, but his friends adored him.

A Stumbling Block

Leo's childhood was happy and simple. He attended school in his neighborhood and spent his free time playing soccer with his friends, brothers, and cousins. He was always surrounded by his family.

When all seemed to be well for Leo, an obstacle presented itself. At the age of eleven he was diagnosed with a growth hormone disorder. Doctors were concerned that without treatment, his growth would be stunted and he would not reach his ideal height.

At an age when most children think only of playing and having fun, Leo had to suffer from injections of drugs into his legs every night. It was rather painful period, witnessed by many friends and family members. The painful treatment continued for several years, night after night. With an unusual maturity and responsibility for a child his age, Leo accepted it.

The Monument to the Flag is a symbol of the city of Rosario, the birthplace of Lionel Messi.

Tough Times, Tough Decisions

The treatment for Leo's condition was very expensive, and there came a point where his parents were unable to afford it. It became necessary to find other means to pay for the medicine. Leo's parents sought

help outside Argentina. Relatives in Lérida, Spain, offered a helping hand. His father found work there and Leo received the opportunity to try out for FC Barcelona. It was a moment of change. By leaving home, Leo would be able to broaden his horizons and in every sense of the word, he was able to grow.

> As if he had never left, in Lionel Messi's hometown everyone keeps him in mind and remembers him playing ball on the sidewalk.

The decision for the family to settle in Barcelona was really difficult, but it was Leo's enthusiasm which motivated the Messi family to follow through with the decision.

CHAPTER 2

Arrival at Barcelona

LEO MESSI ARRIVED AT BARCELONA WITH HIS FATHER on September 17, 2000. He was 13 years old, had the ability to move the ball, and had the unconditional love of his family. Besides that, there was nothing else. In addition, he needed to seek medical attention. Father and son reached the hotel and unpacked their suitcase.

Although today it looks rather easy to take a plane and cross the ocean, but for a working family like the Messis, this was not an easy decision. His mother and siblings stayed behind in Argentina. Leo had to leave them behind, along with his neighborhood and the small things that made him such a happy child.

Leo and his father left, knowing that they had exhausted every last resource in Argentina. The treatment was impossible because it was too expensive. Perhaps they could find help in Spain.

Leo urgently needed to solve his health issues. When he would go out on field to perform his magic with the ball, he looked like a child two or three years younger than his actual age. That is to say, although he was thirteen, he had the size of a ten-year-old child. When Leo played, his opponents seemed to be enormous and their legs endless. Today he says that challenge allowed him to develop agility, quickness, and ball skills that other player did not have.

The Opportunity

Barcelona is a really beautiful city. Any recent newcomers would take a stroll and take pictures here and there. But Leo and his father were not tourists. They had a very clear purpose.

The day after he arrived in Barcelona, Leo presented himself to the FC Barcelona team for a tryout. His playing skills and stature managed to draw the attention of the club coaching staff. He played and the height difference from the rest of the players was so remarkable that it appeared that he was in the wrong category. However, his playing skills were greater than his size.

A few days later, the coach responsible for signing contracts offered Leo his first contract. He confirmed that the club would take care of Leo's medical expenses. The trip had been worthwhile.

Leo Messi signed his first contract on a paper napkin. There the head coach of FC Barcelona confirmed that the club (team) agreed to incorporate him into the lower divisions of the club and take care of his medical treatment. Today Leo still keeps that old napkin and says it is one of his fondest treasures. At the time, many members of the club's leadership did not understand why one of the team managers wanted to recruit a 13-year-old Argentinean boy. When they personally met Leo, they believed it was a bad joke. The child was actually very small and they could not understand how he could be a prodigy with the ball. However, once they saw Leo play they would not let him go—hence his first contract was signed on the first piece of paper they could find at hand, a paper napkin.

When Leo joined FC Barcelona in 2003, Frank Rijkaard was his first coach.

Polishing Raw Talent

For three years, between 2000 and 2003, Leo played and trained on the youth FC Barcelona team. The goal of the coaches was to transform this rough diamond into a jewel that could shine at the European Championships.

Though his father was with him, the rest of the family had stayed in Rosario. At FC Barcelona the daily routine was hard and constant work. It was not like neighborhood soccer. It required discipline and rigor to play for one of the most recognized clubs in Europe. Little by little, Leo's hard labor began to bear fruit.

In 2003, Leo was the subject of conversation in the locker rooms and hallways of the club. Coaches had witnessed in 2000 a short Argentinean boy quietly seeking an opportunity and needing help. Three years later, this teenager had become the ace in the sleeve of the coaching staff at FC Barcelona. It had been only three years, but Leo was ready to put on a Barca jersey and take the field.

Leo's mother, grandmother, and brothers returned to Rosario because it was very difficult for them to leave their roots at home.

The Great Debut

It was time to go out and show what could be achieved by discipline and training. Leo had reached a physical development more appropriate for his age and maturity, both in life and on the field, which were equally exceptional. One characteristic that attracted the coaches' attention was his humility and meekness. He took the game rather seriously for a boy his age. He was a magician with the ball, but was very humble when praised. When someone congratulated him, Leo simply thanked him with a smile and nothing more.

After competing at the youth level, November 16, 2003, was his big day. On that date Leo played a friendly match

Young Lionel was proud to be compared with the great Diego Armando Maradona.

made him immensely happy. Everything was going just fine.

With his style of work, FC Barcelona had allowed for his best to shine. He had transformed into a great young player, but still felt like he had something to prove for the team that had given him so much.

A Blue and White Passion

In 2005, Leo had an opportunity that he had dreamt about for years. The coach of the Argentine national team invited him to join the team to play in the FIFA World Youth (under 20) championship.

In the very same year, he had already been compared to Diego Maradona, which made him blush. He was only 17 years old, and already had great promises of a championship. He had every reason to boast of his talent, but being meek and modest is his trademark.

Leo exploded in the 2005 U20 World Cup, which was played in Holland. His left foot gave soccer fans a reasons to talk. For Leo, playing in the blue and white jersey of Argentina was a dream come true.

That U20 World Cup gave him much joy. Leo raised the trophy as champion of the tournament, helping Argentina win the final against Nigeria, 2-1. He was also the top scorer of the tournament with six goals, and he won the Golden Boot. The Dutch chain NOS gave him the Golden Ball, an award given base on the audience preference.

against FC Porto. A year later, on October 16, 2004, he wore the club's jersey in an official match against RCD Espanyol. Their highly anticipated debut in European competition was on December 7, 2004, in the Ukrainian club stadium Shakhtar Donetsk. This was not just any match: it was the qualifying match for the Champions League.

On May 1, 2005, Leo made his first goal as a professional player. He was only 17 years and thus became the youngest player who had ever made a goal for FC Barcelona in the Spanish League.

Thanks to Leo's success, his entire family was able to move to Barcelona, which

Lionel Messi avoides a group of Nigerian defensemen during the final of the FIFA World Youth Championships in 2005, won by Argentina.

Leo fights for the ball during a World Cup match.

CHAPTER 3

New Challenges

Lionel Messi's success in the U20 World Cup made headlines around the world. He was only 18 years old, and people were starting to treat him like a superstar. Great players and coaches are familiar with the havoc that such pressure can cause a young player. But after having tasted the glory, how does one get up the next morning and move forward?

After his performance during the 2005 U20 World Cup in the Netherlands, it was clear that the best clubs in the world would be happy to have him. Therefore, FC Barcelona extended his contract until 2010 and ended all discussion about his moving elsewhere. The club knew it could commit to a player with the professional approach of Leo Messi.

Playing to Win the Spanish League

In 2005, Leo obtained citizenship from Spain, of course without abandoning his Argentinean citizenship. Obtaining the Spanish citizenship status allowed him to enter the registry of the Royal Spanish Football Federation (RFEF) and play as a member.

The press repeats one word, which characterizes Leo: speed. The speed at which he controls the ball and moves across the field is unprecedented. His rivals are unable to keep up with him and when they even they try, they fall. It is impossible to stop him.

FC Barcelona took full advantage of his speed to wins the Spanish League Cup in the 2004-05 season and again in the 2005-06 season. But this would be just the beginning for Leo. Everyone knew he wanted more.

Leo helped FC Barcelona win the UEFA Cup in Paris, May 2006. The team defeated Arsenal, 2-1.

The Super Cup of Spain

FC Barcelona fans are celebrating. Each event is a celebration full of magic and goals. Goals which Leo celebrates hugging his teammates and looking towards the sky thanking his maternal grandmother, Celia. The Super Cup of Spain brings face to face the winner of the Spanish League with the winner of the King's Cup. Since FC Barcelona won the Spanish league in con-

secutive seasons, Leo had his first opportunity to fight for, and win, the Super Cup of Spain. But it would not be the last time. He would have the opportunity to do it again in subsequent years.

Argentina National Team

Leo had shown that despite his youth, he was ready to face major challenges. His ability to keep his head out of the clouds, even at times when he was so heavily praised, made most people believe he was a player who could be trusted.

Jose Pekerman, the coach of Argentina's national team, the Albiceleste, knew that Leo wanted to play in the jersey of Argentina. He also knew that playing on the national team is a dream that all Argentinean players want to achieve. Although Leo was still a teenager, Pekerman decided to call him to the squad. He wanted to see him play with the older players, in order to observe how he reacted on the field. On August 17, 2005, Leo played against Hungary. On September 3, he faced Paraguay in a critical game. It was a qualifier for the World Cup, which would be held in Germany in 2006.

Germany 2006

The Argentine national team had a dream

> Leo's humility was always his hallmark trait. He was only 18 when his name was synonymous with soccer around the world.

team. Leo was accompanied by soccer stars who knew how to play on European fields. Carlos Tevez, Juan Pablo Sorin, Esteban Cambiasso, and Hernan Crespo were just a few internationally renowned Argentinean players on the team for the World Cup. But Leo was the one that everyone wanted to see on the field.

In Germany 2006, Argentina qualified out of Group C with two wins and a draw. The Albiceleste won its first game in the knockout round over Mexico, 2-1. However, in the quarterfinal Argentina and Germany were tied 1-1 at the end of regulation time. Germany advanced on a penalty shootout.

The sixth-place finish was a disappointment, but Leo became one of the youngest players ever to score a goal in the World Cup tournament.

The 2007 Copa América

Leo had demonstrated in Germany that he knew how to play with his countrymen and that together they could do really big things. The following year, the coach invited him to take the field with the white and blue once more.

In the 2007 Copa América tournament, Argentina demonstrated their superiority in game after game. They thrashed the

Members of the Argentinean national team (La Albiceleste) pose for a photo before their quarterfinal match at the 2006 World Cup in Berlin.

Despite obtaining Spanish citizenship in order to develop his career in Europe, in his heart Leo has always worn the blue and white jersey of Argentina.

had hoped for more.

A Barca Hero

United States, put Colombia in check, and dominated Paraguay in the third match they played.

But the best was yet to come. In the quarterfinals against Peru, the Albiceleste had an explosion of goals that left the score at 4-0. Soon after, Argentina faced Mexico, winning 3-0, which sent them to the finals. Argentina was one step away from the Cup and Leo was part of the dream.

The Brazilian and Argentinean national teams clashed on July 15, 2007. This classic South American event captivated the two countries. No one could miss the final. However, this time Brazil was better than Argentina, defeating them 3-0.

The finals ended with a very bitter taste for Argentina. Even though he was named the best young player of 2007, Leo was not satisfied. It was a nice recognition, but he

During 2006 and 2007, Leo suffered injuries from which he recovered without difficulties. These did not dampen the brightness of his game. He had many memorable moments with Barca, but a few in particular will forever remain in the hearts of fans.

In March 2007, the Flea scored three goals in a game considered one of the classic rivalries of Spanish football: FC Barcelona versus Real Madrid. Each goal made the Barca fans go crazy, although the game ended in a tie.

Leo is very grateful for those years of which the club opened the door and gave him a chance when he was still a promise. FC Barcelona gave a helping hand in those years when it seemed impossible to pay for medical treatment, they stayed with him and gave him encouragement. In those years, Leo returned the gesture as best he knew how: by showing his greatness on the field. Fans of FC Barcelona were satisfied with his performance in every game.

In 2007 Lionel created Leo Messi Foundation. This project started from the Messi family and aims to help children with different needs fulfill their dreams. Leo's other charitable work includes serving as a UNICEF Ambassador. He has collaborated with initiatives of this organization in Haiti, Spain, Argentina, Costa Rica, and other countries. He is always ready to help. Leo enjoys every charitable action he undertakes. This project relies on international brands that trust him and offer their support wherever he goes.

Leo in an attempt to score for the blue and white.

Bejing 2008

The 2008 Olympic Games were held in Beijing, China. The world stopped to watch a sporting festival that brought together the best athletes in each sport. The opening ceremony was seen by approximately four billion viewers.

The Argentina national team was present and Leo could not have been any happier to have the opportunity to put on the national team's jersey once again. He knew it was in a unique moment in his career and wanted to put all his talents to the service of his native country.

Argentina reeled off a succession of victories—defeating Ivory Coast 2-1, Australia 1-0, Serbia 2-0, and Holland 2-1—to reach the semifinals. On August 19, 2008, the Argentine national team faced Brazil in a rematch of the 2007 Copa América final. This time, Argentina came out on top by a 3-0 score. The Albiceleste were in the final, ready to take on Nigeria to fight for the gold medal. On August 23, 2008, Argentina beat the African team by a score of 1-0. Leo had accomplished his mission by helping Argentina win an Olympic gold medal.

Leo making magic with the ball.

CHAPTER 4

Captain

BY THE FALL OF 2008, 21-YEAR-OLD LEO HAD ALREADY accomplished things on the soccer field that others could only dream of. Around the world, he was being compared to many of the greatest players of soccer. With Barca and the Albiceleste he had performed legendary plays and scored noteworthy goals. But new challenges awaited young Leo.

For FC Barcelona jersey number 10 has special meaning. That number has been worn by some of Barca's most legendary players. Before Leo joined the team, the number had worn by Ronaldinho. Before him, Maradona, Romario, Rivaldo, Hugo Sotil, Luis Suarez, and many other great players wore the number 10 for the club.

FC Barcelona was very much alive during the 2008-09 season as well as the 2009-10 season, it was if they were a story of heroes. Leo has reached his peak and it showed on the scoreboard and the standings. On August 3, 2008, he would wear jersey number 10 of FC Barcelona. Though he had the pleasure of lifting the cup of the Spanish League before, this time it was different. Now he could do it as captain.

5,000

At this point in his career, Leo seemed unstoppable on the field. He plays forward position. His rivals are not going to let Leo get away from them and try their best to keep up with him. Leo continues ahead and has a vision of the field and a speed that does not allow for anyone to approach him. When everything seems to have failed and his oppo-

nents in desperation attempt to stop him by means of strategies outside of the usual regulations, such as pulling his shirt or strong kicks. However during this time in his career, Leo does not know barriers, he only knows goals.

On February 1, 2009, Leo scored another goal for Barca. But this was a different goal—one that had special meaning for the club and its fans. It is the 5,000th goal scored in the history of the club. Chants, shouts, hugs, celebrations, confetti, and of course, a cheer that vibrates to the fans that are in the stadium and those who watch the team from their homes.

The King's Cup

The Cup is a highly valued prize in the Spanish championship. Top Spanish clubs compete for it each year in a knockout tournament. This championship is organized by the Royal Spanish Soccer Federation.

Spain is a country where the monarchy is an important cultural asset. The Cup is a championship, where the best of the best appear. At the end, His Majesty King Juan Carlos I, personally delivers the cup to the champion. The event is truly unique. To receive this majestic cup from the Spanish monarch's own hands is not something that

In 2009 Leo won the Gold Ball and was named Best Player in the World by FIFA.

Although Leo is characterized by his "devilish" left foot, his game possesses great versatility and he always presents a great challenge to his opponent.

happens every day. Leo raised the Cup in Mestalla Stadium when FC Barcelona defeated Athletic Bilbao on August 23, 2009.

UEFA Cup
Champions League

Some of the competitions organized by UEFA are the most prestigious media for soccer. Among them is the UEFA Champions League. This tournament invites the top clubs from Europe and is one of the most anticipated sporting attractions for soccer fans worldwide.

In 2009 FC Barcelona defeated Manchester United 2-0 in the UEFA Cup final for the Champions League. Leo scored one of the team's two goals. It was a long cherished dream and it had come true. When reporters approached Leo and asked how he felt, he replied that he was the hap-

In 2008, a brand of sportswear chose Leo to tell his life story and to relate it to the slogan "Nothing is Impossible." Leo explained that his growth problems as a child would eventually make him a better soccer player. Leo described himself and showed how he perceived his opponents. The difficulties that he encountered on the soccer field when his opponents were much larger than him forced him to develop his ball-handling skills. Being smaller made him more agile than others, and he had to learn to play soccer close to the ground. The story shows a person who was able to overcome a major life challenge and transform it into an area of strength.

Leo on the attack during a World Cup qualifying match against Peru.

piest man in the world. Many were happy for him, his family, and his country. Very true to his personality, Leo said no more and went out to celebrate. He was a champion and had been chosen by fans as the best player in the tournament and he was crowned top scorer with nine goals. Shortly thereafter he received the 2009 Golden Ball as the season's best player.

South Africa 2010

Leo's plays and goals planted and harvested titles. He was unstoppable and gave FC Barcelona all his talent. But the Argentina senior team summoned him. The appointment was in South Africa 2010 and Diego Armando Maradona was the squad's new head coach. All eyes were on Leo, who was considered the star of the team. Everyone wanted to see how this player, who performed miracles in Europe, would do in South Africa.

Argentina won its three matches in group play, defeating Nigeria 1-0, the Republic of Korea 4-1, and Greece 2-0. In the knockout round, Argentina ended

Mexico's hopes with a 3-1 win. But the dream of Argentina was shattered in the quarter-finals, the Albiceleste was were defeated by Germany, 4-0. Once again, the Argentines returned home with a bitter taste in their mouths and an unfulfilled dream of World Cup glory.

Winning Spain's Super Cup Once Again

Leo and his team were once again among the best in La Liga during the 2009-10, 2010-11, and 2011-12 seasons, and that gave them a ticket to contend for the Super

> When he is performing at his best, Lionel Messi is a creative player who has an extraordinary technical skill with the ball.

Cup of Spain again. In the 2009-10 season Barca won against Athletic Club Bilbao. In the following season, FC Barcelona came face to face with Sevilla FC, and won again. In the 2011-12 season, again Leo and FC Barcelona had a third chance to defend their titles, this time against Real Madrid. Behind Leo, Barca remained the Super Cup champions.

In the 2009-10 season, Leo won prizes such as the Golden Ball, FIFA World Player trophy scorer, and Golden Boot Achievements that no one else has been able to achieve to date.

Leo is a relentless player that makes the playing field into what others consider impossible. His speed and skill with the ball makes his moves seem cartoon worthy and not those of an actual player. The teenager who arrived at FC Barcelona looking for an opportunity seems to be a collector of titles and trophies.

In the 2009-10 season, Leo scored 34 goals in 68 games for Barca and won the Golden Boot.

Leo scores for FC Barcelona during the 2011 King's Cup tournament.

CHAPTER 5

Moving Forward

LEO'S LIFE IS AN UNFINISHED STORY, but even today it is a beautiful one. He is 24 years old, still studies the ball and concentrates on the next game. The camera flashes have not changed who he is. His family has been his strongest support and things that once seemed an obstacle are now behind him.

Leo plays with a responsible joy. He exhibits a flattering humility and a shyness that is not common in an elite athlete who has achieved so much. Being a superstar does not seem to affect him. He has grace on the soccer field and his level of concentration in extreme situations enables him to make magic.

Volunteer Work

Though his soccer career occupies most of his time, Leo is committed to less fortunate children. He has channeled his interest in helping those most in need through his own nonprofit organization, the Leo Messi Foundation. This is a personal initiative being overseen by his family. The foundation aims to give a hand to children at risk so they may have the opportunity to fulfill their dreams.

In addition, Leo has been named Goodwill Ambassador for UNICEF and collaborates with various organizations in solidarity and humanitarian tasks in Argentina, Spain, and the rest of the world.

A Fan Favorite

Leo has won the hearts of fans of FC Barcelona. However, those who saw him grow and started games out of the ball as a child, remember him most fondly. His primary school classmates,

"I know there are a lot of children that have diseases, many that don't have an education, many that don't have good nutrition. I am ready to do everything I can to help them in my collaboration with UNICEF," said Leo when appointed a UNICEF Goodwill Ambassador in March 2010.

friends of Grandoli and Newell's Old Boys, Rosario neighborhood residents speak of him with emotion.

Reports say that Leo was an energetic child who did not like studying and always wanted to win. He was a good teammate, a leader in the recess and an adored grandson by his maternal grandmother. They say that it was she who discovered his talent with the ball and took him for the first time to the neighborhood club. Leo dedicates his goals to his grandmother and admits that in his greatest moments of joy he shares them with her.

Leo visits his native hometown Rosario whenever he gets the chance and walks the streets of his neighborhood as any normal person. He greets people; give autographs and poses for a bulk load of photos. Getting in touch with his roots feeds and gives him strength to keep going.

Compared to Other Greats

Leo's greatness encourages many journalists to compare him with soccer legend Diego Armando Maradona. Both were considered to be the best players of their times. Both played for Barcelona and the Argentine team wearing the number 10. But such comparisons are unfair. Messi and Maradona each seem to keep that in mind, every time the press stalks them with such questions: Is Messi the new Maradona? What do they have in common?

Leo's family has always accompanied him. This has given him the support he had needed to face new challenges.

How do they differ? Is Messi better than Maradona? Is Maradona better than Messi?

Leo takes the comparison as a compliment. He recognizes that Maradona has already established his own prominent place in soccer history, and that he still has a long career ahead of him. When asked such questions, Leo always tries to show

Barcelona players celebrate winning the league championship at the Nou Field, Barcelona, May 2011.

Despite having won major victories with Barcelona, Leo says it has always been an honor for him to play in the white and blue jersey of Argentina.

On many occasions he has spoken in support of Messi and expressed his admiration and concern for the young star.

A Unique Talent

Leo does not mistreat the ball. It appears at times that a web of rivals is going to take the ball by assault, but he only needs to give it a strong kick. The ball jumps with grace and finesse and enters the goal. He taps the ball and it responds with physics-defying stunt. It has been said that Lionel Messi knows how to perform miracles with the ball.

As a player Leo has accomplished many things. Despite his youth, today he is considered to be one of the greatest players in soccer history. Sometimes, rival defenemen lose their patience and use methods that go beyond the regulations in order to try to stop him. When Leo falls down, he gets right back up and continues to attack. In his life Leo has learned that, due to his size, there will always be obstacles. However, he knows that nothing is impossible. He just gets back up and gives his best.

his respect and appreciation for Maradona and his accomplishments.

For his part, Maradona knows that the pressure of wanting to be the best can wreak havoc in the head of a young player.

No one doubts that even if Leo were to retire from professional soccer right now, his name would be written right next to the giants of the sport. Only being 24 years old, he has already collected numerous titles and awards, placing him on the top. His humility lets us know one can always go further and that to improve oneself should be the ultimate goal. His solid work habit demonstrates his willingness to be there for those who are less fortunate and in need of help. His unconditional love for his hometown and his country makes him a wonderful example for his countrymen. Talent, humility, and solidarity seem to define his profile.

FURTHER READING

Leonardo Faccio. "Messi". Buenos Aires: Debate, 2011.

Leonardo Faccio. "Messi: The Guy Who Was Always Late (and Today is First)." Buenos Aires: Debate, 2011.

Luca Caioli. "Messi: The History of the Boy Who Became a Legend." Barcelona: Salsa Book, 2011.

Luca Caioli. "Messi: The Boy Who Could Not Grow." Barcelona: Salsa Books, 2008.

Sergio Barbui and Pablo Lafourcade. "The History of Argentine Football." Buenos Aires: Planeta, 2011.

INTERNET RESOURCES

http://www.leomessi.com

Official website of Lionel Messi. The site includes information about his career, his life, calendar of events, press, etc.

http://www.fcbarcelona.es/

The official site of the club FC Barcelona. There you can find information about the club and its various sports teams.

http://www.canchallena.com/

A digital sports publication of the Nation Group, an Argentinean multimedia company.

http://www.afa.org.ar/

This is the official site of the Argentina Football Association. It contains information on the national teams, competitions, news, regulations, etc.

http://www.fifa.com/

Official site of the Fédération Internationale de Football Association (FIFA), the governing body of international soccer.

INDEX